Becoming A Pioneer

Becoming A Pioneer

A Book Series

The Month-by-Month Guide
to Doubling Your Business and
Taking Over Your industry in a Year

Bimal shah

Book 2: Resolve your Biggest Challenge.

Becoming a Pioneer - Book 2
© Copyright 2022 by Bimal Shah

ISBN: 978-0-9909014-6-4 Paperback

ISBN: 978-0-9909014-5-7 Hard Cover

TheOneYearBreakthrough.com

For more information, email: Bimal@theoneyearbreakthrough.com

Rajparth Achievers, LLC
55 N.E. Fifth Avenue, Suite 402
Boca Raton, FL 33432

Connect with Pioneers around the World. Every Month. With the book purchase, you are a member. No strings attached.

Join Me and walk away with personalized insights for you in the monthly Club meeting.

Get Your **Free Membership** here

https://bit.ly/ThePioneersClub

Learn Exponentially More.

This book is best used in conjunction with this training that allows you to not only resolve your biggest challenge, pain, or frustration but also make a big leap in your business goals.

Get Your **Free Video Training** at

https://bit.ly/TheChallengeResolver

Dedication

To my wife Ami and our daughters, Rajvi and Parthvi. This book would not have been possible without the efforts of my wife Ami with the editing. Her strength and support is priceless. Also, I am indebted to my daughters for invaluable insight on the structure and design. My family is everything to me.

I love them with all my heart.

Contents

Author's Preface

Making Pioneers! —The What and Why

What is a Pioneer?

A pioneer is unique and different from the rest.

To be a pioneer, you need to be the Only One at something. This book is about breaking all the barriers and obstacles you have in your life, work, habits, and mindset. The purpose of this book is to bring a 10x to a 100x transformation in your perspective about your own self—to assist you in realizing your true potential in a very short time.

Why be a Pioneer?

God has made every human being unique and different. When every human becomes unique and different, the whole world can work in harmony. Becoming a pioneer happens through stages and discoveries. I wrote this book with the intent to create the essential stages and discoveries you will need at each step. Drawing from my own experiences, it builds fresh perspectives that can take your business to the next level.

Editor Ami Shah with Author Bimal Shah.

Introduction

How to get the most out of this Book Series

Go slow. This is a book that you do not want to read fast. Write in the book, scribble in it, make notes, have sticky notes with you. Carry this book with you wherever you go. This is your book and customized manual to help you at least double what you believe you can do in a year.

Even if you answer one question from this book, it will have a positive impact in your life or business. Below are five ways you can make the most out of this book:

1. Read first, think second, and then write: Read a sentence or two or paragraph. Think about it and answer the questions that follow.

2. Go digging: Look up something in your business or your personal life related to the question. And then come back and answer the question.

3. Use Sharp Pencils with an eraser on top: Instead of using pens, please use pencils, as while you are writing your thoughts to the questions, the answers may change in due course.

4. Watch the video before you start reading: In the video, you will get a lot more insights about the book itself. It will walk you through powerful elements to scale.

5. Scan the QR CODE and save the QR CODE link in your Notes on your Smartphone: When you answer a specific question, look up the links listed in the Link Tree. See if there is a resource for the problem you are trying to solve. The Link Tree is very useful. It works like magic; you will find new and amazing things each time you look.

Special Advice for Using This Book in Uncertain Economic Times

As we all know, the future is questionable. I recommend using this book series in a sequential order to stabilize and speed up your income growth. Follow the advice in the acronym UNCERTAIN:

U-Unique - Discover from each book how to become unique. Book #5 lists elements to leverage to be unique.

N-New – Apply the different tools and systems taught in book #1, book #9, and book #11. To bring in the new you in record time.

C-Confidence – Use the Confidence Journey tool from book #5. To build daily confidence in your journey.

E-Empathy – Use the Self-Empathy skills from book #10 and book #2 (this one). To deal with uncertainties, biggest pains, or frustrations.

R-Resilience – Lay the foundation for building resilience with a powerful vision in book #1. Apply the Book #12 resiliency skills.

T-Transparency – Discover from book #3, book #4, and book #6 how to use good or bad transparency. This is about you and your business, to propel to the next level.

A-Audacious –From book #1, book #13, and book #6 you will discover how to maintain and chase audacious goals.

I-Implementation – From Book #7 on Sprints and Book #8 on Leadership. Throughout each book in the series, you will become a master implementor. Leaders lead by example.

N-Next Steps – Every single chapter in each book helps you build your customized next steps. There is no way you can't stabilize or grow if you follow all the steps you built by yourself, using this book series.

How to use this Book Series in Prosperous Economic times.

When times are good, you can make it better by using this book series with the acronym AWESOME as follows:

 A-Algorithms - In business when there are a lot of opportunities coming your way, you need to apply an algorithm: a one-line business plan. Build your customized scale from algorithms listed in book #4 and book #13.

W-Wins – At the end of every chapter, you celebrate your wins. In book #5 you have the tools that make it a recurring habit.

E-Extra –There is no traffic beside you in the extra mile. In book #12, you will have the systems to drive on the no-traffic roads.

S-Surprisers –What to do when your team and customers surprise you. You are bound to get surprised quite often. Discover best responses in book #1, book #2 (this book), book #3, book #4, and book #10.

O-Omnipresence –Through book #6 and book #3, you will build your own systems. Through book #11 you will build your own skill sets. Through book #9 you will build the platforms. In book #10 you will have the systems and tools to automate omnipresence.

M-Multiplication –When times are good, you need systems to multiply. Through Book #1 you will lay the foundation for multiplication. Through Book #7 you will build the skills. Through Book #8 and book #9 you will build the traits for becoming a multiplier and systems essential for it.

E-Extinguishers –When things are happening like rapid fire. You will need different kind of extinguishers. This is to extinguish the fires and keep the pace you are moving at. Build your own fire extinguishers from book #3.

Introduction

So many self-development and business books are out there, but this book is unique in the way it incorporates questions that you are going to answer. In that process you will discover your unique self.

This book revolves around one topic that allows you to go deep and make a real positive difference. Even if you spend five minutes reading this book, you will feel the difference. The uniqueness about this book is that this series, you will cherish forever. It has your Goals, Plans, Actions, and most of all a System you can use every year. The system consists of a series of 13 stages that each lasts 4 weeks. Thus, you can achieve your 3-year goal in one Year. Secondly, I did not want to write anything that you already knew through common sense. There are many questions and tools for you to walk away with practical solutions. As you put them in place, you will see results.

I hope this book will make a highly positive impact in your life. I have left enough space after each question to elaborate your answers in depth.

Looking forward to meeting you in Part III!

Week 1

Frustration, Challenge, and Pain Are Different

I used to think that they were the same—but they are different. I used to look at them in an intermingled way, but they need different approaches and strategy. Now I know that Pain needs relief, Challenge needs strategy, decisions, and action. Frustration needs elimination. Looking at them through those lenses has brought clarity and confidence. It reflects in my actions and decisions.

Many years ago, I thought of my employees as my biggest frustration, challenge, and pain. They were all individuals. My frustration was not getting the daily tasks done my way. My challenge was to get my employees on an accountability system. My pain was their behavior. Once I understood all three and resolved each in a different manner, there was a big transformation in the team. Now they're productive every day. They're my asset now. I overcame my frustration by eliminating tasks and focusing on outcomes—creating a joint strategy to tackle the outcomes. I strategized my challenge by building an accountability system with my team.

Resolving your frustration and challenge leads to productivity and happiness in your life.

The words "frustration," "challenge," and "pain," as I use them in this book, are questions to the reader. The-follow through can help you take necessary steps in resolving each.

Frustration	Challenge	Pain
Something that annoys you, irritates you, and bothers you. This means that this event or situation or consistent behavior is going beyond your tolerance level. Taking care of the frustration will make you more energized and immediately productive.	Something that you are trying to achieve but cannot, and you feel by trying you will improve, get better, become stronger, or learn something from the failure. Overcoming your challenge will make you feel happy—ready to take on another challenge.	Something that creates sadness or inflicts despair or emotional discomfort because you fail to understand how or why or what you can do to relieve this pain. Taking care of this pain will make you feel at peace with yourself and the world.

On the next page you will be able to use the illustrations to build a process of using your frustration, challenge, and pain to discover who needs to do what by when.

Eliminating Frustration in Business:

Frustration in business makes you feel the same way.

Overcoming Challenge in Business:

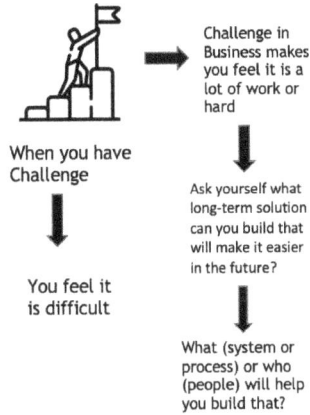

Challenge in Business makes you feel it is a lot of work or hard

When you have Challenge

You feel Angry, Annoyed, Irritated

Aim towards elimination

Ask yourself what long-term solution can you build that will make it easier in the future?

You feel it is difficult

You need to get rid of it

Who or what will help you eliminate it?

What (system or process) or who (people) will help you build that?

Relieving Pain in Business:

Pain in business makes you feel hurt

When you Have Pain

Ask yourself what situation got you that pain?

You need Relief

What (system or process) or who (people) will get you relieved from that pain?

With this is mind, now turn to the questions that follow in this book. Apply them to as many challenges, pains, or frustrations as you might have. Whenever you change or improve something, that's when you see a difference. So, if you want to speed up your results, look at everything that frustrates you. Also, look at things that challenges you or cause you pain. Change something about the problem immediately, and don't be afraid to fail.

Failure is a part of the success formula. If you want to double your success, quadruple your failures. That doesn't mean you want to fail or that you go into situations unprepared. There's a formula for failing successfully Let's look at your situation and how you can fail successfully or come out successful and not fail at all.

What is one area in life you are not moving forward in because you are afraid of failure?

_____

_____

_____

Does that failure meet the following three principles?

Will you fail fast? ☐ Y ☐ N

Define fast for you: (one week, one month, three months, etc.)

_____

_____

Will you fail forward? ☐ Y ☐ N

Define Forward for you: (Example: "It will open up so many doors for me." "I will make more money" or "I will be more skilled in new capabilities.")

_____

_____

Will you fail small in terms of money? ☐ Y ☐ N

Define small for you in financial terms:

_____

_____

If that failure meets all three of these conditions—failing fast, forward, and with little financial loss—you are ready to embark on it, no longer fearing failure. If you are indecisive and don't want to decide, or if you decide not to go forward with it (thus, not to move on to other things), in that scenario you will still have to deal with these frustrations in life and work. Your frustrations will become a boomerang. So, let's deal with it right now.

What is your Biggest Frustration or pain or challenge?

_____

_____

_____

_____

_____

What is your current approach to deal with that frustration, pain, or challenge?

_____

_____

_____

What are the top three obstacles or roadblocks that are preventing you from resolving that frustration or biggest pain or biggest challenge in the first place?

1._____

_____

_____

_____

2._____

_____

_____

_____

3._____

_____

_____

_____

What are the top three strategies that can deliver the highest payoff and resolve that frustration, pain, or challenge?

1. _____

_____

_____

_____

2. _____

_____

_____

_____

3. _____

_____

_____

_____

What are the top three triggering actions or habits that are causing that frustration or biggest pain or biggest challenge in the first place?

1. _____
   _____
   _____
   _____

2. _____
   _____
   _____
   _____

3. _____
   _____
   _____
   _____

Ask yourself: "What are the three steps I can take to change those actions or habits?"

1. _____
   _____
   _____
   _____
   _____

2. _____
   _____
   _____
   _____
   _____

3. _____
   _____
   _____
   _____
   _____

Ask yourself, "What are the top three decisions I make on a regular basis that cause that frustration or biggest pain or biggest challenge to develop?"

1. _____
   _____
   _____
   _____

2. _____
   _____
   _____
   _____

3. _____
   _____
   _____
   _____

Ask yourself, "What do I need to change in my thinking process for each of the three decisions, so I can make better decisions next time?"

1. _____
   _____
   _____
   _____
   _____

2. _____
   _____
   _____
   _____

3. _____
   _____
   _____
   _____

Ask yourself, "What is working in each of the three actions or habits that cause the frustration, pain, or challenge?" (Chances are, nothing is working, or, maybe some pieces of the actions are working for you, while some aren't.)

1. _____
   _____
   _____
   _____
   _____

2. _____
   _____
   _____
   _____
   _____

3. _____
   _____
   _____
   _____
   _____

Ask yourself, "What's not working in each of the three actions or habits that cause the frustration?"

1. _____
   _____
   _____
   _____
   _____

2. _____
   _____
   _____
   _____
   _____
   _____

3. _____
_____
_____
_____
_____

Knowing what you know now, if you were to start all over again, what are the top one to three things you would have never started at all?

1. _____
_____
_____
_____

2. _____
_____
_____
_____

3. _____
_____
_____
_____

How will you get out of those things you should have never started and how soon?

1. _____
_____
_____
_____

2. _____
_____
_____
_____
_____

3. _____
   _____
   _____
   _____
   _____

Knowing what you know now, if you were to start all over again, what are the top one to three things you would have done differently to get a better result?

1. _____
   _____
   _____
   _____
   _____

2. _____
   _____
   _____
   _____
   _____

3. _____
   _____
   _____
   _____
   _____

What are the top three things you need to stop?

1. _____
   _____
   _____
   _____
   _____

2. _____
_____
_____
_____
_____

3. _____
_____
_____
_____
_____

What are the top three new things you need to start?

1. _____
_____
_____
_____

2. _____
_____
_____
_____

3. _____
_____
_____

What are the top three new things you need to scale? By scaling in this context, I mean you can exponentially grow a specific outcome or area. For example, if you had never written a blog and you wrote a popular first blog, you can now decide to write one every week or thrice a week, thus, "scale" it.

1. _____
_____
_____
_____

2. _____
_____
_____
_____
_____

3. _____
_____
_____
_____
_____

Who needs to do what by when to successfully implement those steps?

Who	What	When

Many a time, frustrations happen, maybe because you have fundamental issues on how you approach business or life. For example, you may get frustrated with employees who don't do what you want to get done. The fundamental problem there is how you train or hire your team.

Do you feel you have got a grasp on the difference between your Pain, Challenge, and Frustration? And why each is essential to Scale?

❏ Y ❏ N

You can scale each one as follows:

Pain: You may feel pain from having difficult conversations with your employees about awkward situations. But afterwards, you feel relieved. Now you scale them by having a system to courageously keep having conversations.

Challenge: You may feel challenged to embrace technology in your business, but you embrace it, learn it, and hire experts to train you in it. Now you scale it by adapting many different technologies or technological platforms in your business.

Frustration: You may be frustrated by having no accountability from your team members. Now you build a system to have it with one of your key team players. It works. When you implement that accountability with many other team members, you are scaling it.

Now you are ready to answer the question above. If yes, that's great. You can put financial numbers to each of these goals and envision the possibilities.

If not, please see if you can qualify for a complimentary workshop by scanning the QR Code and select Free Workshop. I've developed helpful tools and workarounds, including a unique hiring process, as well as providing talent management.

You shortchange yourself by thinking small and giving up. Work towards whatever comes your way, and you will get through it. Now it's time to make God proud of your daily achievements next . . .

P.S: Don't forget to check out the free resources on the next page before you move to the next chapter.

Useful Resources

QR Code to scan and get all Free Tools and Resources:

Link from the QR Code:

https://linktr.ee/TheOneYearBreakthrough

Link to all my events:

https://www.eventbrite.com/o/bimal-shah-7943115300

Your Chapter Takeaways

Your Biggest Pain

_____

_____

_____

_____

Your Biggest Challenge

_____

_____

_____

_____

Your Biggest Frustration

_____

_____

_____

_____

How you will solve each of those puzzles

1. _____

   _____

   _____

2. _____

   _____

   _____

3. _____

   _____

   _____

Your Transformation: _____

_____

_____

Time to Celebrate

Before you jump to the
next chapter, take some
time to Celebrate.

Below are five simple small ways you can celebrate:

1. Catch up on your favorite series.

2. Plan a dessert outing at an authentic dessert place

3. Go watch a movie at a cinema.

4. Watch the Sunset.

5. Enjoy Tazo® Tea! (One of my favorites!).

Week 2

Make God Proud of Your Daily Achievements

I used to for a long time go with the flow. It is not a good way to go about your day. Then one day, I asked myself the question "Instead of the day happening to me, how can I happen to the day?" I know that when you ask that question at the beginning of the day and commit to those few victories, it transforms. Now let's learn how you can do the same! About five years ago, I used to think that you can manage time and achieve this or that. But it boils down to managing your mindset. That's when all my transformation began. Things started progressing. I also had a special relationship with God. I treated God as a friend and not someone I feared. When you make God your friend, God will provide you direction, and you will make the right decisions. You will not stop doing the wrong things from a fear of consequences, but by choice. And that is so much powerful and everlasting.

My personal experience is that God rewards in different ways when you work hard towards your goals and do the right thing. God is always unconditionally loving but I had several instances that when I work at something very well, the results make me proud. This is how I feel God is proud of my achievements. For example: I worked hard during the crisis of the pandemic. I con-

21

sistently adapted, pivoted, changed, learned, and improved to build new avenues for income. By doing so, I had the best year ever and exponentially grew my business.

This was unbelievable; the prayers and hard work paid off. God shows his pride with his support. When you look upon God as a trustworthy friend and faith, God will be supportive.

This week, you're going to learn how to make your loved ones proud of you—by allocating time and transforming your frustration, pain, or challenge into ideal situations. Allocating blocks of time for important things in life and business is essential. This achieves and accelerates your breakthroughs. This way, you are in control of your time. Instead of time controlling you. The only way to make that shift is to understand your priorities and work on them. To understand your priorities, you must use your imagination about your ideal future. Imagine ideal scenarios and work towards them to understand what you need to focus one. So that's what we will work on this week.

What block of time throughout the day or week are you currently allocating to work on resolving that biggest pain or challenge or frustration?

_____

_____

_____

_____

_____

_____

If you can't allocate time, what are the top three truths (not excuses) that are preventing you from successfully allocating the block of time needed to resolve your biggest pain, challenge, or frustration?

1._____

_____

_____

_____

_____

_____

2._____

_____

_____

_____

_____

_____

3._____

_____

_____

_____

_____

_____

What is your current daily time-management system?

Your Morning Routines to Get you fully charged:

_____

_____

_____

_____

_____

Your Work Routines to be effective at work every day:

_____

_____

_____

Your Bedtime Routines to have a regular good night's sleep every day:

_____

_____

_____

Now that you have built the routines, you are ready to make every day a great day. Please follow the steps in the illustration on the next page to make every day amazing.

As an entrepreneur, what you do with your time changes everything

Your list of things to do seem endless

Too much gives you too much stress

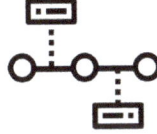

Solving the mystery of time management is in the time itself. It is staring right at us and yet we don't see it - Different blocks and routines make it a great day.

MaKe TODaY AMazing

When you make every day amazing, you make God Proud of you.

Imagine you had a magic wand. When you wave it, the frustration, challenge, or pain magically disappears. It converts into an ideal situation. What does that situation look like? Describe it in detail:

_____

_____

_____

_____

_____

_____

_____

_____

_____

_____

What three biggest elements are different from the current situation that's causing pain, frustration, or challenge?

1. _____

_____

_____

_____

_____

2. _____

_____

_____

_____

_____

3. _____

_____

_____

_____

_____

What are the top three actions you need to take to make those three missing elements materialize in your life?

1. _____
   _____
   _____
   _____
   _____

2. _____
   _____
   _____
   _____
   _____

3. _____
   _____
   _____
   _____

If you don't know what actions you need to take or how to take them, think who can help you make those elements become a reality.

Who	Cell Phone	Website	Email	Date you will contact

What would be the biggest difference it would make in your life if those three elements were in it?

_____

_____

_____

_____

_____

_____

What would be the biggest difference in your workplace if those three elements were in it?

_____

_____

_____

_____

_____

By When would you like the ideal scenario to appear?

_____

Why is this ideal scenario important to you?

_____

_____

_____

_____

_____

What financial resources do you need to commit to get those three elements into your reality?

_____

_____

_____

_____

_____

_____

Do you currently have those resources? ☐ Y ☐ N

If yes, that's great. By what date will you commit those financial resources?

_____

If No. How will you acquire those financial resources?

_____

_____

_____

Will you have to borrow money at unfavorable rates? ☐ Y ☐ N

If Yes, Stop. Look for alternate ways to generate capital. How much do you need to make from your customers to generate that capital?

$_____

Ideally, how many customers should it take to generate that sum?

_____

Who is your "Ideal" Customer?

What name would you like to give to your ideal customer? _____ What are the demographics of your ideal customers? What are their sociographic, psychographics? How do they spend their day? Where do they eat? What do they read? Where do they shop? Where do they go to have fun? (If you are not familiar with the terms demographics, sociographics, or psychographics, "demographics" mean the customer's factual attributes: age, sex, race, income, married status, etc.; "psychographics" is the emotional factors: why they buy, the values they attach to products; "sociographics" is their hobbies, passions, etc.)

_____

_____

_____

_____

_____

_____

_____

_____

_____

_____

_____

_____

_____

_____

_____

_____

_____

_____

_____

_____

_____

What are the top three places you would find your ideal customer
_____ (name) Online?

   1. _____
      _____
      _____

   2. _____
      _____
      _____

   3. _____
      _____
      _____

What are the top three places you would find your ideal customer
_____ (name) Offline?

   1. _____
      _____
      _____

   2. _____
      _____
      _____

   3. _____
      _____
      _____

What are the top three networking places you would find your
ideal customer _____ (name) Offline?

   1. _____
      _____
      _____

   2. _____
      _____
      _____

   3. _____
      _____
      _____

Do you belong to all three networks? ☐ Y ☐ N

If no, by when will you join those networking groups?

_____

What are the top 10 names or connections who can get you to your ideal customer?

1. _____
   _____
   _____

2. _____
   _____
   _____

3. _____
   _____
   _____

4. _____
   _____
   _____

5. _____
   _____
   _____

6. _____
   _____
   _____

7. _____
   _____
   _____

8. _____
   _____
   _____
   _____

9. _____
   _____
   _____

10. _____
_____
_____

What are the biggest frustrations your "Ideal" Customer has in working with people like you or people who are not nearly as good as you?

_____

_____

_____

_____

_____

_____

_____

_____

_____

What Keeps your "ideal" customer awake at night or concerned when working with people like you?

_____

_____

_____

_____

_____

What Keeps your "ideal" customer frustrated with you or people like you?

_____

_____

_____

_____

_____

_____

_____

_____

_____

_____

_____

What are the top three actions you need to take to improve your customer service to your ideal customers?

1. _____
   _____
   _____
   _____

2. _____
   _____
   _____
   _____

3. _____
   _____
   _____

Now convert all your thoughts into actions and figure out who needs to do what by when:

Who	What	When

What are the conversations your "Ideal" customers have in their head with themselves before they want to meet you or even think about utilizing your services? What do they think about before they even want to consider your services?

_____

_____

_____

_____

_____

_____

_____

_____

_____

_____

_____

_____

What are the top three ways you will capitalize on this conversation through online messages, emails, or posts?

1. _____
   _____
   _____
   _____
   _____

2. _____
   _____
   _____
   _____
   _____

3. _____
   _____
   _____
   _____
   _____
   _____

What are the top three ways you will capitalize on this conversation through offline mailers or messages?

1. _____
   _____
   _____
   _____
   _____

2. _____
   _____
   _____
   _____

3. _____
   _____
   _____
   _____
   _____

Now convert all your thoughts into actions and figure out who needs to do what by when:

Who	What	When

Getting back to those three elements, what are the time commitments you will have to make for each of the three elements?

Element that you need to commit time for	How much time will it need?	Date and time you have allocated on your calendar for the same	Result that you want to achieve in that time frame	Next Step

In the next page, I am providing an implementation tool that will be very useful for you in executing anything in life and business.

The Implementation Guarantor™

Prepared For_____

Start Date: _____   End Date: _____

Results that you want to Achieve	Who?	What Specific Action needs to be taken to achieve that result?	By When?	Review Date?

The Implementation Guarantor™

Prepared For _____

Start Date _____   End Date _____

What are the obstacles, opposition or challenges you faced?	What Solutions will you implement to overcome those?	Result Achieved and By When

Many a time, your dreams don't come true because you have fundamental issues on how you approach business or life. For example, you may have business goals, but your operations are in disorder and without proper structure. You may be providing instructions on the fly and your team is asking you 10 times more questions on the fly, taking your time away from productive, profitable activities. The fundamental problem there is how you provide training and development. One bigger problem than most other problems could be how your office culture is at work. You may need to develop better culture and values at work. Many of our CEO clients have seen better culture develop very rapidly through some unique tools and exercises that we have shown them. You can discover some of them when you scan the QR Code on the next page.

Do you feel you have got a great grasp on how you can make it a great day every day?

☐ Y ☐ N

If yes, that's fantastic. You are now ready for the next step—to make those Belief Systems a foundation for your daily actions, decisions, rituals, and habits. Look at your B.S. (Belief System) that stands in the way. And/or the one that can pave the way for your success.

If not, please see if you qualify for a complimentary workshop by scanning the QR Code and selecting "Free Workshop."

You shortchange yourself by not going the extra mile. There is very little traffic in the extra mile. One of the reasons you may not go the extra mile is because of your own B.S. Let's discover that next.

P.S: Don't forget to check out the free resources on the next page before you move to the next chapter.

P.P.S: Don't forget to celebrate!

Useful Resources

QR Code to scan and get all Free Tools and Resources:

Link from the QR Code:

https://linktr.ee/TheOneYearBreakthrough

Link to all my events:

https://www.eventbrite.com/o/bimal-shah-7943115300

Your Chapter Takeaways

Your Top 5 Daily Routines that will make you become your best possible self!

1. _____
2. _____
3. _____
4. _____
5. _____
6. _____

Your Top 5 Daily Habits that you need to Change (Replace)!

1. _____(old)
   _____(new)
2. _____old)
   _____(new)
3. _____(old)
   _____(new)
4. _____(old)
   _____(new)
5. _____(old)
   _____(new)

Time to Celebrate

Before you jump to the
next chapter, take some
time to Celebrate.

Below are five simple small ways you can celebrate:

1. Do 10 Burpees. It will get your heart rate pounding.

2. Breathe 2X in and 4X out—3 to 5 times.

3. Go give a hug to a family member.

4. Play hide 'n seek for a few minutes.

5. Plan an outing for a day.

Week 3

Belief Systems That Will Make You Succeed

What is your interpretation of B.S.? I view it as "Belief Systems"—even the slang nonsense you call B.S. I reframe as Belief Systems. I used to think that all my beliefs were a foundation to success. But to my surprise, I found out that a few of my B.S. were a big impediment to my success—and in fact the foundation for my failure.

I was so adamantly convinced of some of the beliefs that I became headstrong until my wife asked me one question. She asked, "Who put that belief in your head?" At that moment, I did not have a clear answer. I tried tracing the answer to that question, and I could not find the source. Whether it was friend, relative, parents, family members, google, books, or experience. I realized that it is your own B.S. that gives you success or failure.

If it was Experience, I would try to recollect that experience. Paint it from beginning to end and view it in the context of the current situation. If it made Sense, I would stick with that belief. How would I drop it? I would say to myself: It's my B.S. If it was a friend or relative, I would ask myself, how did they get that B.S. in their head?

This week, we are going to work with your mindset and your Belief System: Belief Systems that prevent you from being successful. Understanding what your mindset is doing for you is key. That is an effective way of making a change in your mindset.

With the biggest pain and frustration you identified earlier, what is your state of mind when you usually deal with that pain or frustration?

_____

_____

_____

_____

_____

_____

_____

_____

_____

_____

_____

_____

The biggest positive impact you can make on your state of mind is by making a positive impact on your body. The more physical activity you do, the better your state of mind will be always.

How do you currently get physically charged and energized to take control of your day?

_____

_____

_____

_____

_____

_____

_____

_____

If you are currently not doing any physical activity that gets your brain fully charged, then that is the first thing you should implement. If you start your day with your phone fully charged at 100 percent, why do not you charge yourself at 100 percent when you start your day.

What are the top three physical activities you will do to charge your brain with full energy?

1. _____

   _____

   _____

2. _____

   _____

   _____

3. _____

   _____

   _____

People start building beliefs based in what they associate themselves with and their identities. You are what you think you are. Over the next pages I will illustrate when to change your beliefs—and how to find your identities that work and eliminate those that don't.

Weak
Identities

Strong Identities

Belief Systems
that don't work
for you

Belief Systems
that work for
you

Change

Improve

Based on the preceding illustration, please use the questions that follow to discover your foundational identities and build the belief systems that can really help you grow.

What are the top ten identities you associate yourself with (positive or negative? Be honest with yourself.) (Example: I am shy, I am an introvert, I am forgetful, I am fat, I am . . .)?

1. _____
   _____
   _____

2. _____
   _____
   _____

3. _____
   _____
   _____

4. _____
   _____
   _____

5. _____
   _____
   _____

6. _____
   _____
   _____

7. _____
   _____
   _____

8. _____
   _____
   _____

9. _____
   _____
   _____

10. _____
    _____
    _____

Out of the Top 10 identities you discovered above, what top three identities that you have associated with cause the biggest pain or frustration in your life or business?

1. _____
   _____
   _____

2. _____
   _____
   _____

3. _____
   _____
   _____

Out of the top 3 identities you have associated yourself with, how has that improved the situation that's causing the biggest pain or frustration in your life or business?

_____
_____
_____
_____
_____
_____
_____
_____
_____

Knowing what you now know, what are the top three identities you will eliminate and replace to achieve a better outcome in the situation that's causing the pain or frustration?

Identities I will eliminate:

1. _____
   _____
   _____

2. _____
_____
_____

3. _____
_____
_____

Identities I will replace them with:

1. _____
_____
_____

2. _____
_____
_____

3. _____
_____
_____

What are the action items I need to take to implement these identities?

Who	What	When

What are the top ten belief systems (core values) you associate yourself with (positive or negative—Be honest with yourself) (Example: I cannot do presentations, I can close effectively, I can't speak in front of a crowd.)

1. _____
   _____

2. _____
   _____

3. _____
   _____

4. _____
   _____

5. _____
   _____

6. _____
   _____

7. _____
   _____

8. _____
   _____

9. _____
   _____

10. _____
    _____

Out of the Top 10 belief systems you discovered above, what are the top three belief systems you have identified with that cause the biggest pain or frustration in your life or business?

1. _____
   _____

2. _____
   _____

3. _____
   _____

Out of the top 3 belief systems you have identified with, how have they helped you in the situation that's causing the biggest pain or frustration in your life or business?

_____

_____

_____

Knowing what you now know, what are the top three belief systems you will eliminate and replace to achieve a better outcome in the situation that is causing the frustration?

Belief Systems I will eliminate:

1. _____
   _____

2. _____
   _____

3. _____
   _____

Belief Systems I will replace it with:

1. _____
   _____

2. _____
   _____

3. _____
   _____

What are the action items I need to take to implement these belief systems?

Who	What	When

Regarding the biggest challenge you identified earlier, what is your state of mind when you usually deal with it?

_____

_____

_____

_____

_____

Out of the Top 10 identities you listed earlier, what are the top three you have associated with that cause you the biggest challenge?

1. _____
   _____
   _____

2. _____
   _____
   _____

3. _____
   _____
   _____

Out of the top 3 identities you have associated, how have they helped you resolve the situation that's causing the biggest pain or frustration in your life or business?

_____

_____

_____

_____

_____

_____

Knowing what you now know, what top three identities will you eliminate and replace to achieve a better outcome in the situation that's causing the pain or frustration?

Identities I will eliminate:

1. _____
   _____

2. _____
   _____

3. _____
   _____

Identities I will replace them with:

1. _____
   _____

2. _____
   _____

3. _____
   _____

What are the action items I need to take to move into these identities?

Who	What	When

Out of the Top 10 belief systems you identified earlier, what are the top three belief systems you have associated with that cause you to face the biggest challenge?

1. _____
   _____
   _____

2. _____
   _____
   _____

3. _____
   _____
   _____

Out of the top 3 belief systems you have associated with, how have they improved the situation that's causing the biggest pain or frustration in your life or business?

_____
_____
_____
_____
_____
_____

Knowing what you now know, what are the top three belief systems you will eliminate and replace to achieve a better outcome in the biggest challenge you are facing?

Belief Systems I will eliminate:

1. _____
   _____

2. _____
   _____

3. _____
   _____

Belief Systems I will replace them with:

1. _____
   _____

2. _____
   _____

3. _____
   _____

What are the action items I need to take to implement these B.S'?

Who	What	When

Your mindset does not shift because of core fundamentals in life and business. For example, you may have a habit of overexaggerating each opportunity you get, only to discover the opportunity is not even a tenth of what you imagined. This brings disappointment, and you make rash decisions. Through our platform and training you can access our systems. It helps you check every opportunity in terms of its value to your business. There is 12-Step Business Fundamental system that allows you to scale your business. It is available to our Scale members for free.

On the contrary, you may have a habit of over-worrying. Something that looks bad on the surface may not be as bad as you think.

Do you feel you have a good grasp on how you can use your B.S. to achieve improved levels of success, even rise to the next level?

☐ Y ☐ N

If yes, that is great. You are now ready to build a rock-solid system for powerful habits to achieve your 3-year goal in One Year in the next chapter . . .

If not, please look at a complimentary workshop and see if you qualify. To do so, please scan the QR Code and select "Free Workshop."

You get stuck because of your B.S., and you can get Free because of your B.S. When you have Freedom, you can scale. The choice is yours. Once you have your beliefs down to a T, you will need rock-solid habits that you can build on. Let us build those now . . .

P.S: Do not forget to check out the free resources on the next page before you move to the next chapter.

P.P. S: And do not forget to celebrate!

Useful Resources

QR Code to scan and get all Free Tools and Resources:

Link from the QR Code:

https://linktr.ee/TheOneYearBreakthrough

Link to all my events:

https://www.eventbrite.com/o/bimal-shah-7943115300

Your Chapter Takeaways

Your Top 5 B.S. that you need to Eliminate!

1. _____
   _____
   _____

2. _____
   _____
   _____

3. _____
   _____
   _____

4. _____
   _____
   _____

5. _____
   _____
   _____

Your Top 5 B.S. that you will never let go of, as they make you who you are and a Pioneer:

1. _____
2. _____
3. _____
4. _____
5. _____

Time to Celebrate

Before you jump to the
next chapter, take some
time to Celebrate.

Below are five simple small ways you can celebrate:

1. Make a smoothie!

2. Go bicycling for a brief time—it is very relaxing.

3. Ask Google a funny question incognito so the cookies do
not follow you everywhere.

4. Share a laugh with your family.

5. Do work around the house.

Week 4

A "Fifth Why" System to Build Powerful Habits

I have always heard of building new habits or changing existing habits, but I could rarely find a system. Is there a method? Is there a structure to do so? Now, after so many attempts, I have developed a system that works. That's what we will talk about here. Let me share a story.

About five years ago, I used to look for ways to improve habits and tried many resources. Then one day, I kept asking, *why?* I asked it over and over—for five times—and each time went deeper. It was on the Fifth time I exclaimed "Hallelujah." When I connected the dots, I realized I had stumbled on a combination of mindset, triggers, the *fifth why,* and the beginning. That's when everything started shifting. That's what you will build this week.

This week you are going to learn how to develop habits: the habits that can assist you in overcoming your biggest challenge. And in resolving your frustration about how to overcome the same. Habits define everything and make you do everything to a degree that you may not even be aware of.

So, let's look at what habits we need to change and what habits we need to leverage.

Please describe or articulate a situation that creates your biggest pain or frustration:

Briefly describe or articulate a situation that creates your biggest pain or frustration:

_____
_____
_____
_____
_____
_____
_____
_____
_____
_____

Now take a moment to circle some words within this description that could be related to your habits and identify the Top 5 habits that you identified:

1. _____
   _____

2. _____
   _____

3. _____
   _____

4. _____
   _____

5. _____
   _____

Now Imagine your highest self (highest you ethically, morally, financially, spiritually, physically, emotionally) as a best friend is sitting down next to you and what he or she would say you ought to do about those habits:

1. _____
   _____

2. _____
   _____

3. _____
   _____

4. _____
   _____

5. _____
   _____

After you identify what habits, you need to work on, we need to create a plan to change them or leverage them to make you a better You. Habits don't change overnight. Make your journey to changing your habits much easier with the process on the next page. You will feel peaceful, happy, productive, and even profitable!

Let's get started.

What are the triggers that cause you to behave the way you behave in each one of those habits?

1. _____
   _____
   _____
   _____

2. _____
   _____
   _____
   _____

3. _____
   _____
   _____
   _____

4. _____
   _____
   _____
   _____

Once you understand the triggers, you can understand the root cause of why this is happening and make the essential changes to your behavior and habits. Without going to the root cause, it can take you very long to change your habits, perhaps even a lifetime.

What root cause creates the trigger that activates your behavior? (If you are unable to get to the root cause right away, ask WHY five times and go to the FIFTH WHY; you will get to the root cause. Please read the example on the next page to understand how to get to the FIFTH WHY)

1. _____
   _____
   _____
   _____

2. _____
   _____
   _____
   _____

3. _____
   _____
   _____
   _____

4. _____
   _____
   _____
   _____

5. _____
   _____
   _____
   _____

(If you can get to the root cause right away, you can skip reading below and move on to the next set of questions. However, reading the next page will give you an excellent insight on how the FIFTH WHY can help you in many situations in life and business.)

Example of FIFTH WHY:

Ask yourself the WHY question Five Times to understand the main reasons that are preventing you from reaching a goal—that are in opposition to that success.

Example: You have not attained the sales goal of $1 Million that you have been trying hard to get to. You ask yourself what obstacles have been preventing you from getting there. So, you make a list of obstacles and oppositions. Below is an example of some of them:

1. I don't have enough leads.

2. People aren't buying my product.

3. My price is higher than the competition's.

4. Prospective customers don't seem to have a need for my product.

5. I don't have enough capital.

Now you would take each one of the obstacles and ask yourself the question WHY five times on each one. Let's take the first example—not having enough leads.

1st Why: The first time you ask that question, your mind may say: *I don't have a huge database.* To overcome that, you may think about increasing the database and devise strategies for the same.

2nd Why: On the second why, you may ask, "Why do I need a bigger database?" Or "Why don't I have a bigger database?" The mind may respond *I don't need a bigger database but instead I need to improve my message.* Or this time, the mind may respond *I don't have the money for database building or the resources to market that database anyway.* Then you look to another solution and investigate improving your message.

3rd Why: Now you ask, "Why do I need to improve my message to my customers?" When you ask that, you may find that the answer is, you need to create better value than your competitors and make them feel that you understand them.

4th Why: Now perhaps you ask, "Why do I need to make them feel understood?" When you ask that question, your mind may say: *Your message makes them feel you understand them. That will make them buy from you at the price you ask.*

5th Why: Now, for the fifth why question, you might ask yourself why the customers will be willing to pay the price you ask for. At this point, your mind may say the answer is that they can't find your unique product or service anywhere else. To make that answer real, you must make your product or service unique. Give them what they desire rather than what you may deem they need.

From the above example, you can see how going deep actually solves many problems. It solves problems across different layers in the company. Going all the way to the *fifth why* solved the problem of the price, the competition, the capital, the need for the product, and the desire to buy the product. Going deep in understanding the root cause can create many "a-ha" moments in your brain. At the same time, you may also discover some "oops" elements you need to change.

Once you identify the reasons for trigger points in your behavior, it's time to create a solution: a desirable environment in your mind or in your work or living space. It will deter the trigger points from developing.

You are now ready to use the illustration on the next page to build improved habits for next-level personal and professional growth.

The Fifth Why

GO DEEP

Better Habits

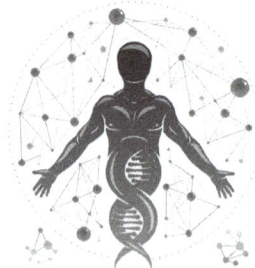

Better You and Better Business

What changes do you need to make in your environment?

You need to establish what the trigger points are, understanding what triggers your mind to habitually take certain decisions and your body to act accordingly. That will prevent each of the trigger points from being set off.

1. _____
   _____
   _____
   _____

2. _____
   _____
   _____
   _____

3. _____
   _____
   _____
   _____

4. _____
   _____
   _____
   _____

5. _____
   _____
   _____
   _____

As a result of learning about these triggers, what new behavior will you commit to in order to make yourself a better business leader, parent, spouse, and overall, a better human?

1. _____
   _____
   _____

2. _____
_____
_____
_____

3. _____
_____
_____
_____

4. _____
_____
_____
_____

5. _____
_____
_____
_____

Now, it takes 21 times of doing it consistently to make a new habit. So, the next step is to practice these new behaviors. Your commitment is what will create this dramatic change. To have that commitment, you need to have a bigger purpose and goal that you are achieving. First, define that goal in your mind. Or you may incentivize yourself by putting something at stake.

Let me share a quick story. In 1997, I incentivized myself to attain an impossible goal by risking something huge. It was my very first year after college. I had decided I wanted to make six figures and be in the top three agents with Northwestern Mutual Life Insurance Company in the region, and if I didn't reach that goal, I would quit, shave off my moustache (which I was very proud of), and never be an entrepreneur again. Everyone said it was an impossible goal, as in the past no one had done it without a strong professional background, like being an accountant or lawyer, and with a lot of clients. I did it in my very first year straight out of college, becoming #2, the youngest ever in the region, honored in

Sports Illustrated and *Time* magazine with my moustache on! I have been a thriving entrepreneur ever since.

Please use The Habits Implementor™ tool on the next page to build better habits.

	The Habits Implementor™ Prepared For: _____	Start Date: _____ End Date: _____
New Habit that I will Implement	**Incentive if I do this Habit for 21 consecutive times**	**Something I lose or commit to do that I hate to do If I don't do this consistently**

The Habits Implementor™		Start Date: _____
Prepared For: _____		End Date: _____

Track record of dates of me doing it consistently for 21 times.

1 ___/___/___	2 ___/___/___	3 ___/___/___	4 ___/___/___	5 ___/___/___	6 ___/___/___
7 ___/___/___	8 ___/___/___	9 ___/___/___	10 ___/___/___	11 ___/___/___	12 ___/___/___
13 ___/___/___	14 ___/___/___	15 ___/___/___	16 ___/___/___	17 ___/___/___	18 ___/___/___
19 ___/___/___	20 ___/___/___	21 ___/___/___			
1 ___/___/___	2 ___/___/___	3 ___/___/___	4 ___/___/___	5 ___/___/___	6 ___/___/___
7 ___/___/___	8 ___/___/___	9 ___/___/___	10 ___/___/___	11 ___/___/___	12 ___/___/___
13 ___/___/___	14 ___/___/___	15 ___/___/___	16 ___/___/___	17 ___/___/___	18 ___/___/___
19 ___/___/___	20 ___/___/___	21 ___/___/___			
1 ___/___/___	2 ___/___/___	3 ___/___/___	4 ___/___/___	5 ___/___/___	6 ___/___/___
7 ___/___/___	8 ___/___/___	9 ___/___/___	10 ___/___/___	11 ___/___/___	12 ___/___/___
13 ___/___/___	14 ___/___/___	15 ___/___/___	16 ___/___/___	17 ___/___/___	18 ___/___/___
19 ___/___/___	20 ___/___/___	21 ___/___/___			
1 ___/___/___	2 ___/___/___	3 ___/___/___	4 ___/___/___	5 ___/___/___	6 ___/___/___
7 ___/___/___	8 ___/___/___	9 ___/___/___	10 ___/___/___	11 ___/___/___	12 ___/___/___
13 ___/___/___	14 ___/___/___	15 ___/___/___	16 ___/___/___	17 ___/___/___	18 ___/___/___
19 ___/___/___	20 ___/___/___	21 ___/___/___			
1 ___/___/___	2 ___/___/___	3 ___/___/___	4 ___/___/___	5 ___/___/___	6 ___/___/___
7 ___/___/___	8 ___/___/___	9 ___/___/___	10 ___/___/___	11 ___/___/___	12 ___/___/___
13 ___/___/___	14 ___/___/___	15 ___/___/___	16 ___/___/___	17 ___/___/___	18 ___/___/___
19 ___/___/___	20 ___/___/___	21 ___/___/___			

Now do the same exercise for your biggest challenge and your biggest pain.

Briefly describe or articulate your biggest challenge and why this is such a challenge. What situation or situations cause it to be the biggest challenge?

_____

_____

_____

_____

_____

_____

_____

_____

Now take a moment to circle some words within your description that might relate to your habits. Then write down the Top 5 habits that you identified:

1. _____

   _____

   _____

   _____

2. _____

   _____

   _____

   _____

3. _____

   _____

   _____

   _____

4. _____
   _____
   _____
   _____

5. _____
   _____
   _____
   _____

Now Imagine your highest self (highest *you* ethically, morally, financially, spiritually, physically, emotionally) as a best friend is sitting down next to you and what would he or she say you ought to do with those habits:

1. _____
   _____
   _____
   _____

2. _____
   _____
   _____
   _____

3. _____
   _____
   _____
   _____

4. _____
   _____
   _____
   _____

5. _____
   _____
   _____
   _____

Now that you have identified what habits you need to work on, let's create a plan. A plan to change them or leverage them to make you a better You. Habits don't change overnight. Please follow the process outlined on the next page. Your journey to changing your habits will become much easier, which will make you feel peaceful, happy, productive, even profitable!

Let's get started.

What are the triggers you experience that cause you to behave the way you do in each one of those habits?

1. _____
   _____
   _____
   _____

2. _____
   _____
   _____
   _____

3. _____
   _____
   _____
   _____

4. _____
   _____
   _____
   _____

5. _____
_____
_____
_____

Once you understand the triggers, you can understand the root cause of why this is happening and make the essential changes to your behavior and habits. Without going to the root cause, it can take you a very long time to change your habits, perhaps even a lifetime.

What is the root cause that creates the trigger that creates your behavior? (If you are unable to get to the root cause right away, ask WHY five times and go to the FIFTH WHY; then you will find out the root cause.)

1. _____
_____
_____
_____

2. _____
_____
_____
_____

3. _____
_____
_____
_____

4. _____
_____
_____
_____

5. _____
_____
_____
_____

Now that you identified the root cause of the trigger points in your behavior, it's time to create an environment in your mind or in your physical work or living space to prevent the trigger points from arising.

Making changes in the environment in your living space or work-space can prevent the trigger points from developing. For exam-ple, let's say you have papers on your desk that you haven't looked at in a while, or the desk is completely disorganized—that doesn't make you think better; on the contrary, your thoughts are getting impacted. But suppose instead you had only a yellow pad on your desk—nothing else. You were working on writing down what you imagined as your dream-come-true customer and building an ideal profile. Your phone was silent for 90 minutes, and you were com-pletely focused. You had tasty coffee or tea right next to you. After 90 minutes, the result you got was the best result you've seen in years. The environment makes a huge difference.

For each of the trigger points, what are the changes you need to make in the environment that will prevent each of the trigger points from developing?

1. _____
   _____
   _____
   _____

2. _____
   _____
   _____
   _____

3. _____
   _____
   _____
   _____

4. _____
   _____
   _____
   _____

5. _____
   _____
   _____
   _____

As a result of these changes, what new behavior will you commit to that will make you a better business leader, better parent, spouse, and overall, a better human?

1. _____
   _____
   _____
   _____

2. _____
   _____
   _____
   _____

3. _____
   _____
   _____
   _____

4. _____
   _____
   _____
   _____

5. _____

_____

_____

_____

Please use The Habits Implementor™ tool on the next page to build better habits.

	The Habits Implementor™	Start Date: _____
	Prepared For: _____	End Date: _____

New Habit that I will Implement	Incentive if I do this Habit for 21 consecutive times	Something I lose or commit to do that I hate to do If I don't do this consistently

| The Habits Implementor™ | Start Date: _____ |
| Prepared For: _____ | End Date: _____ |

Track record of dates of me doing it consistently for 21 times.

1 __/__/__	2 __/__/__	3 __/__/__	4 __/__/__	5 __/__/__	6 __/__/__
7 __/__/__	8 __/__/__	9 __/__/__	10 __/__/__	11 __/__/__	12 __/__/__
13 __/__/__	14 __/__/__	15 __/__/__	16 __/__/__	17 __/__/__	18 __/__/__
19 __/__/__	20 __/__/__	21 __/__/__			
1 __/__/__	2 __/__/__	3 __/__/__	4 __/__/__	5 __/__/__	6 __/__/__
7 __/__/__	8 __/__/__	9 __/__/__	10 __/__/__	11 __/__/__	12 __/__/__
13 __/__/__	14 __/__/__	15 __/__/__	16 __/__/__	17 __/__/__	18 __/__/__
19 __/__/__	20 __/__/__	21 __/__/__			
1 __/__/__	2 __/__/__	3 __/__/__	4 __/__/__	5 __/__/__	6 __/__/__
7 __/__/__	8 __/__/__	9 __/__/__	10 __/__/__	11 __/__/__	12 __/__/__
13 __/__/__	14 __/__/__	15 __/__/__	16 __/__/__	17 __/__/__	18 __/__/__
19 __/__/__	20 __/__/__	21 __/__/__			
1 __/__/__	2 __/__/__	3 __/__/__	4 __/__/__	5 __/__/__	6 __/__/__
7 __/__/__	8 __/__/__	9 __/__/__	10 __/__/__	11 __/__/__	12 __/__/__
13 __/__/__	14 __/__/__	15 __/__/__	16 __/__/__	17 __/__/__	18 __/__/__
19 __/__/__	20 __/__/__	21 __/__/__			
1 __/__/__	2 __/__/__	3 __/__/__	4 __/__/__	5 __/__/__	6 __/__/__
7 __/__/__	8 __/__/__	9 __/__/__	10 __/__/__	11 __/__/__	12 __/__/__
13 __/__/__	14 __/__/__	15 __/__/__	16 __/__/__	17 __/__/__	18 __/__/__
19 __/__/__	20 __/__/__	21 __/__/__			

Because we are not open-minded or open to change or open to improvements. many a time, habits don't change. Our mind is programmed to think negatively and replay all the news and messages that appear everywhere. If we open ourselves to new possibilities, the only problem that exists is the one we see when we look at ourselves in the mirror. Coaching, Planning, and Accountability are the three founding principles that are essential to great habits, and I have built my entire products and system around those founding principles. To find out more, visit www.TheOne-YearBreakthrough.com

Do you feel you have got a great grasp on building a system to develop great new habits and improve existing ones?

❑ Y ❑ N

If yes, that's great. You are now ready to eliminate your biggest dangers, the ones that make you get stuck in your path of achieving your 3-year goal in One Year in book # 3 . . .

If not, please see if you can qualify for a complimentary workshop by scanning the QR Code and selecting "Free Workshop."

Your habits make you who you are and can make you who you want to be. Once you have a system to build those habits, you are now ready to eliminate all your dangers and move forward rapidly towards the next level. Let's get rid of those in the next book . . .

P.S: Don't forget to check out the free resources on the next page before you move to the next chapter.

P.P.S: Don't forget to celebrate your small wins!

Useful Resources

QR Code to scan and get all Free Tools and Resources:

Link from the QR Code:

https://linktr.ee/TheOneYearBreakthrough

Link to all my events:

https://www.eventbrite.com/o/bimal-shah-7943115300

Your Chapter Takeaways:

No.	Your top 5 Habits that you will build because of the 5th Why	Your top 5 Triggers or Environment you will build to enforce those habits	Your Top 5 ways to incentivize yourself to build that as a habit
1			
2			
3			
4			
5			

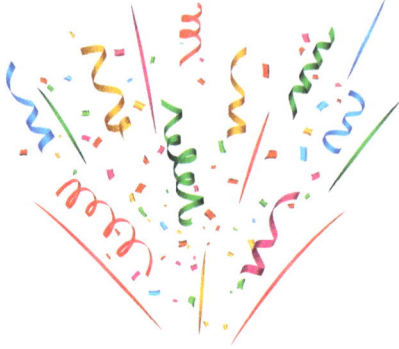

Time to Celebrate

Before you jump to the
next chapter, take some
time to Celebrate.

Below are five simple small ways you can celebrate:

1. Watch a live stage performance.

2. Go Bowling.

3. Retreat into an Escape Room.

4. Try Go-Kart Racing.

5. Spend time in the Pool or Spa!

Doubling Your Business and Taking Over Your Industry in a Year!

Insights from this Book

Below, I have provided proven bottom-line insights from this book to double your business and rise in your industry in a year:

1. Differentiating your Biggest Pain, Challenge, and Frustration:

After you differentiate the three and understand how distinct they are, work on three small steps with a 200 percent growth and elimination of competition in mind.

2. Making God proud of you:

Consider God as a best friend of your highest self and think about a 10X leap you can make in your daily routines. This will double the results you get and make you a pioneer. The fastest way to 2X is to think 10X. Don't worry about failures. Use The Fast, Forward, and small method to fail successfully.

3. B.S. that will make you succeed:

When you look at your belief systems, think about how they will help you grow 200 percent in your business. For example, I need to go narrower and have fewer clients that pay me 3 to 10 times more than the clientele I chase day after day. Identify those beliefs and put financial metrics around those to scale to 200 percent or better. As explained earlier, scale means you do multiples of the same thing. For example, you are successful at making your first video—people love it--and then you decide to do 10, 20, or 100 videos.

4. A "Fifth Why"—a system to build powerful habits:

Going deep instead of shallow makes all the difference. It allows you to go a million miles in one direction instead of mile in a million directions. Go to the *fifth why*, which targets exponential growth in your business: 200 percent in one year. Build the triggers, environment, and habits around these goals.

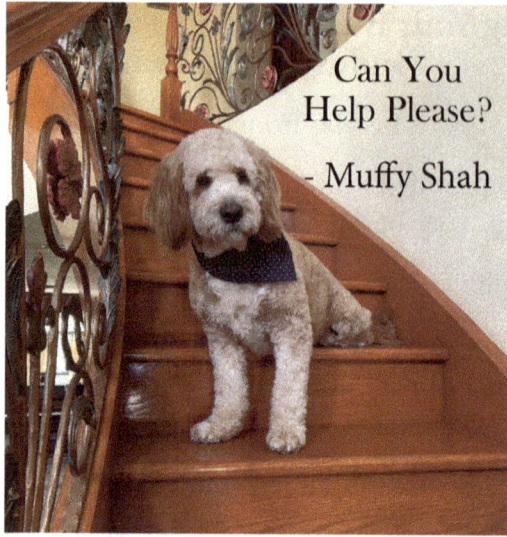

Can You
Help Please?

- Muffy Shah

Thank You for Reading My Book!

I really appreciate it!

I would love it if you can give me an honest review.

I need your input to make my future books better.

Please leave me a helpful, honest 5-Star review on Amazon,
letting me know what you thought of the book!

Thank you so much!

—Bimal Shah.

Please don't forget to check out the next book, which will assist you in resolving your biggest pains, challenges, and frustrations.

It is the next step in the sequence of steps to "Becoming a Pioneer" by achieving your three-year goal in one year.

See you in Book 3!

DON'T FORGET

Join The Pioneers Club for FREE!

With each book, you are Eligible to Join the Club Meeting for Free

Connect with Pioneers around the World—Every Month. With the book purchase, you are a member. No strings attached.

Connect with Me and walk away with personalized insights for you in the Club meeting held every month.

Get Your FREE Membership at:

https://bit.ly/ThePioneersClub

Conclusion

With this, we conclude Part 2 in the series of breakthroughs that we guide you into every four weeks to become a pioneer. In completing this book, you have now finished the second most essential stage of becoming a Pioneer—resolving your biggest pains, frustrations, and challenges. You now have written proof that your questions are more powerful than answers.

Each book series results in you becoming a better you and thus making the exponential progress towards making you a Pioneer. There is no limit to how far you can go. With every conclusion, there is a new beginning, a new chapter in your life. In Book 3 we will go on to a new beginning but continue from where we left off.

Each part is only going to get better, taking you to an exponential level that you could not possibly ever imagine. Build up your imagination to be ready for an amazing acceleration towards becoming a Pioneer.

Looking forward to meeting you in Book 3 . . .

About the Author

Bimal Shah is an accomplished Senior Executive, Entrepreneur, Advisor, Coach, and Results Leader with more than twenty years of success in the financial-services industry. Leveraging extensive experience in growth, entrepreneurship, talent development, financial reporting systems, profitability systems, and processes to scale, he is an asset for companies spanning various industries, sizes, and stages of growth that are seeking expert assistance in bringing their business to the next level. His broad areas of expertise include executive coaching, strategic planning, operations management, scaling, and growth.

As a breakthrough coach, Bimal has successfully helped companies generate growth more than 50 percent in a year and has taken 26 companies to exponential growth in a year. Through his unique hiring process technique, he has helped dozens of companies hire highly qualified C-Level employees. He has worked with more than fifty companies in providing coaching and financial consulting services across an array of industries, including manufacturing, distribution, home health care, communications industry, security systems, and professional services. His unique Coaching-Planning-Accountability system has generated favorable results in record time for CEOs, reducing their working hours in six months, by 35 percent. As a result, CEOs see exponential company growth within a year's time, can hire smart and productive team members at all levels within a few months, and receive the tools to develop effective "out of the box" marketing strategies and messages.

Bimal is also the founder of Rajparth Advisory Group (2005), which provides financial consulting services to entrepreneurs. Prior to founding Rajparth Group, he worked as an independent advisor from 1996 to 2005 through Northwestern and New York Life, helping more than 1000 families preserve their assets, reduce their taxes, increase their income, and create everlasting legacies. During his tenure, he was awarded the highest honor in the industry, The Million Dollar Round Table—Top of the Table Award for six years in a row and Global Corporate Award for Best Life Insurance Agent in the Asian Indian Community.

Bimal has also authored and published his book, *The Daily Happiness Multiplier* now available on Amazon and in bookstores throughout North America. His unique "Success Deck" consists of 52 Workshop Videos and Tools to positively impact anyone's personal and professional life with a single tool each week for 52 weeks. Bimal earned his Bachelor of Commerce in Economics from the University of Mumbai and his Bachelor of Science in Advertising from the University of Florida. He holds a Chartered Financial Consultant, Chartered Life Underwriter, and Certified Advisor in Senior Living from The American College at Bryn Mawr, Pennsylvania.

Some Accolades for Bimal's Work

"Bimal is the big picture guy and he takes us really deep. I might concentrate on one idea that I think is the greatest idea in this world, and Bimal will come back with making us think 10 times bigger and he's got this amazing ability to see opportunity. He lays out a great plan to get to where you want to go and makes it just so attainable. Every entrepreneur with big goals should consider hiring Bimal and if I could have Bimal in my pocket and carry him around at all times that would be great."

— **Mike Barnhill, Managing** *Partner, Specialist ID*

"Before, I was working 70–80 hours a week. Now it is down to 45–55 hours a week. The personal impact of his coaching has allowed me to spend more time with my family. Financial impact has been priceless because of the time saved. If you are struggling, consider hiring Bimal. His books and coaching have helped me plan and organize where I want the business to go. Bimal has also taught me to push my limits and think about things more in detail on why I am doing this."

—Reginald Andre, CEO, *Ark Solvers, Inc.*

"Bimal's books and workshops have further reinforced and enhanced some aspects of my leadership, in that he has brought on a fresh perspective to my role as a leader of the company. In addition to Bimal being a very engaging and energetic personality, he also has an open-minded and unique perspective to making learning a fun-filled experience for my staff, which then adds immeasurable value to my company."

—Terry Sgamatto, *Managing Regional Director, Seeman Holtz*

"I recently took a leap of faith...one that required a consistent amount of convincing myself out of a scarcity mindset and making an investment. It has just been a few weeks and I am very happy with the results of my decision. Under the advisement of Bimal, I have had to make some drastic decisions in my company but have to say overall, even though some were painful, they have all been results-driven and not emotional. I truly appreciate all that Bimal has helped me create in the first few weeks and cannot wait to see what comes next."

—Sarah Martin, *CEO, Experience Epic. LLC*

www.ingramcontent.com/pod-product-compliance
Lightning Source LLC
Chambersburg PA
CBHW071432210326

41597CB00020B/3760